UNDERSTANDING DISEASE

HEART DISEASE

UNDERSTANDING DISEASE

ARTHRITIS

HEART DISEASE

UNDERSTANDING DISEASE

HEART DISEASE

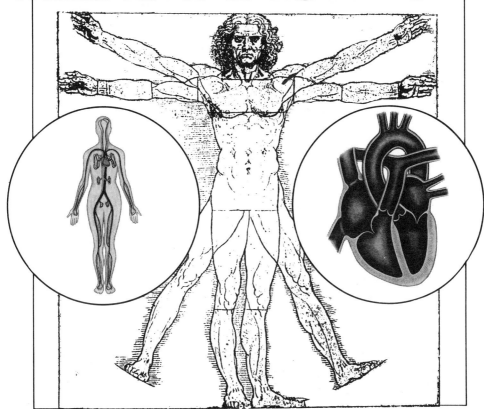

STEVEN TIGER

ILLUSTRATED BY MICHAEL REINGOLD

MEDICAL CONSULTANT: STEPHEN ATWOOD, M.D.

ASSOCIATE PROFESSOR OF CLINICAL PEDIATRICS
COLUMBIA-PRESBYTERIAN COLLEGE OF PHYSICIANS AND SURGEONS, NEW YORK CITY

JULIAN MESSNER 〰 NEW YORK

10 9 8 7 6 5 4 3 2 1

Library of Congress Cataloging in Publication Data
Tiger, Steven.   Heart disease.
   (Understanding disease)
   Includes index.
   Summary: Describes how the heart and circulatory system work and discusses
such problems as heart defects, heart attacks, and other malfunctions. Also
discusses ways of maintaining a healthy heart and treatments for heart disease.
   I. Heart – Diseases – Juvenile literature.   [1. Heart – Diseases]
I. Title.   II. Series.
RC672.T54   1985   616.1'2   85-8949
ISBN 0-671-60021-4

CONTENTS

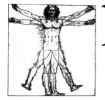# 1: THE NUMBER-ONE KILLER

The number-one killer in the United States is heart disease. In 1982, there were 985,040 deaths from heart disease in this country. By comparison, 435,550 people died from cancer, 95,690 in accidents, 59,980 from chronic lung disease, 50,460 from pneumonia and influenza, and 359,290 from all other causes.

In other words, heart disease kills as many people each year as all other diseases combined.

Over the past ten years, the number of people who die from heart disease has gone down a little. That is probably due to improved treatment methods, and also to the fact that people have started learning how to take better care of their own health. Even so, heart disease remains the single biggest killer, by far.

In the following chapters, we will learn how the heart works, and what happens in different kinds of heart disease. And we'll see how doctors diagnose and treat heart disease. We'll also discuss the efforts being made to prevent heart disease.

Certain kinds of heart disease tend to run in families. With some conditions, the cause is not known. But in the most common kinds of heart disease, a person's lifestyle can be an important factor. What a person eats, how much a person exercises, whether a person smokes – these may be involved in either causing or preventing heart disease.

There has been great progress in treating heart disease. Yet it remains the number-one killer. To change that, people must learn more about what they can do, themselves, to prevent it.

2: HOW THE HEART WORKS

A pump is a machine that moves liquid from one place to another. The heart is a pump, too. It moves a liquid – blood – through a set of channels that run through every part of the body. Without constant movement of blood, we could not live. From before we are born until the moment we die, the heart is working.

The movement of blood throughout the body is called circulation. Like a circle, the blood goes around and around, over and over, constantly pushed along by the pumping action of the heart.

A JOURNEY AROUND THE BODY

Let's follow the blood as it travels through the body. Its job is to bring oxygen and nutrients to body cells and carry away waste products to be eliminated from the body. Therefore, the blood must first go to the lungs, where it will pick up a load of oxygen and get rid of carbon dioxide (one of the waste products from body cells).

The heart is divided into left and right sides. The right side of the heart pumps "used" blood to

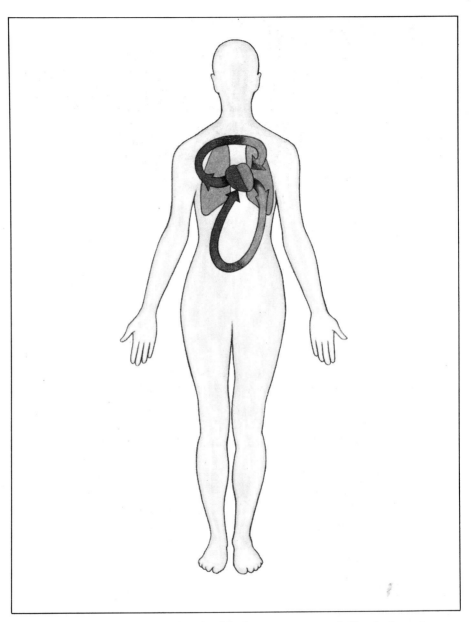

Circulation of the blood. The right side of the heart pumps "used" blood (shown in dark gray) to the lungs. In the lungs the blood dumps carbon dioxide and takes on oxygen. Oxygenated blood (light gray) returns to the left side of the heart, which pumps it to the rest of the body.

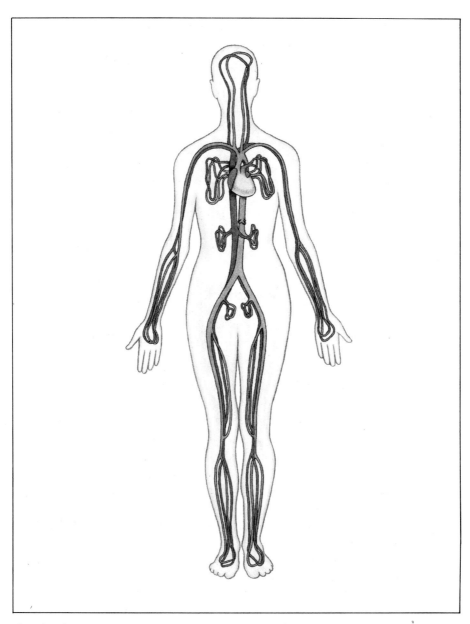

The Circulatory System

the lungs. After that, the freshly oxygenated blood comes back to the left side of the heart, which pumps it through to the rest of the body.

The system of vessels that carry blood from the left side of the heart is like a tree: it starts out with a large trunk called the aorta*, which divides into branches that go to every part of the body. Vessels that carry blood away from the heart are called arteries.

The arteries divide into smaller and smaller branches. The very smallest blood vessels are called capillaries, and they are so small and thin that certain elements in blood can pass right through them. That is how oxygen from the bloodstream reaches the body cells, and how waste products get from the body cells into the bloodstream. All these exchanges take place through the capillaries.

After the blood has delivered oxygen and taken away waste products, it must get more oxygen from the lungs and bring the waste products to the organs that will eliminate them from the body – the lungs and the kidneys.

To reach those organs, the blood must first return to the

heart. From the capillaries, another set of blood vessels – the veins – carries the blood back to the heart. Just the opposite of the arteries, the veins start out tiny and join up with one another, getting larger and larger as they carry the blood back toward the heart. The superior vena cava collects blood returning from all the veins in the head, neck, and arms, and the inferior vena cava collects blood returning from all the veins in the rest of the body.

These two large veins enter the right side of the heart, which will pump the blood to the lungs. Like the aorta from the left side of the heart, one large artery comes from the right side of the heart, and it divides into smaller and smaller branches. This is the pulmonary artery "tree." Finally, the blood reaches the pulmonary capillaries, where it will dump its carbon dioxide into the lungs and take on fresh oxygen. Then the blood returns along a set of pulmonary veins (two from each lung) to the left side of the heart, which will pump it through the body again. A certain amount of blood pumped from the left side of the heart reaches the kidneys, which filter out waste products other than carbon dioxide. Also, a certain amount of blood reaches the intestine, where nutrients are

* Defined in the glossary

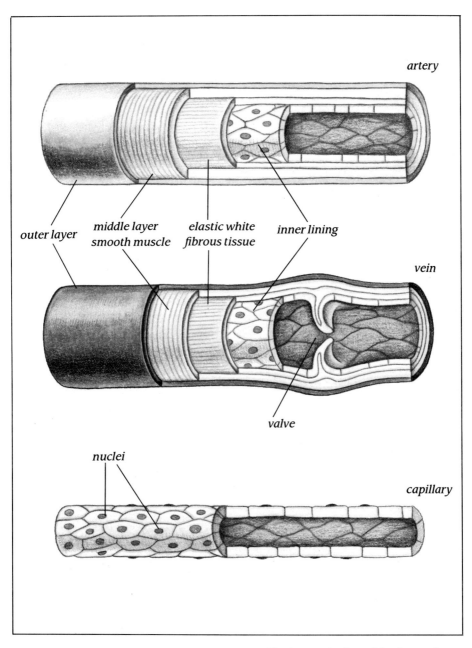

Arteries are thicker and stronger than veins. Capillaries are the finest blood vessels.

absorbed from the food we eat.

In other words, we really have two separate circulatory systems. The pulmonary circulation carries blood from the right side of the heart to the lungs and then returns it to the left side of the heart. The systemic circulation carries blood from the left side of the heart to all other parts of the body and then returns it to the right side of the heart. Each system has its own arteries, capillaries, and veins. And in the middle, forever pushing the blood along, is the heart.

INSIDE THE HEART

There are four chambers in the human heart, two on the right side and two on the left. The right and left sides are separated by a septum (wall) that keeps the "used" blood on the right side from mixing with the freshly oxygenated blood on the left side.

The upper chamber on each side is called the atrium*. Systemic veins bring "used" blood returning from all over the body into the right atrium, while the pulmonary veins bring freshly oxygenated blood returning from the lungs into the left atrium. The atrium passes the blood down to the lower chamber on each side – the ventricle*. The right ventricle pumps blood out the pulmonary artery to the lungs, while the left ventricle pumps blood out the aorta to the rest of the body.

The ventricles are the actual pumping chambers of the heart. (The atria also pump, but only to push blood down into the ventricles.) On each side of the heart, after the blood has passed from the atrium down into the ventricle, the ventricle contracts – that is, the heart "beats" – to push the blood out. To prevent backflow, a valve between the atrium and ventricle permits blood to move in one direction only – forward, from the atrium to the ventricle. On the right side of the heart is the tricuspid* valve, so named because it has three cusps (flaps). On the left side is a bicuspid (two-flap) valve, but it is always called the mitral valve, because it resembles a miter, the split hat worn by a bishop of the church.

When the flaps are down, the valves are open and blood can pass downward from the atria to the ventricles. Then the ventricles start to contract, pushing the blood in all directions, including upward. That pushes up the flaps, closing the valves.

There are two more valves in the heart, one where the aorta arises from the left ventricle and another where the pulmonary

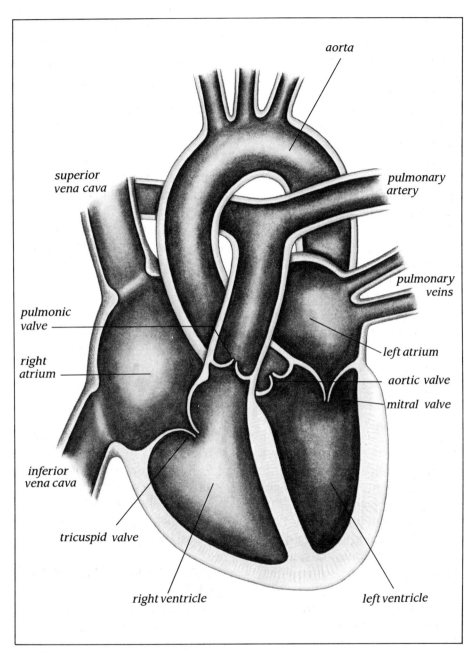

aorta

pulmonary
artery

superior
vena cava

pulmonary
veins

pulmonic
valve

left atrium

right
atrium

aortic valve

mitral valve

inferior
vena cava

tricuspid valve

right ventricle

left ventricle

The Structure of the Heart

artery arises from the right ventricle. These valves serve the same function as the mitral and tricuspid valves: to prevent blood from moving backward. As the ventricles contract, the aortic and pulmonic valves are pushed open so that the blood can get out of the heart.

THE CARDIAC CYCLE

Let's look at the whole sequence, starting with the left ventricle contracting. As it starts to contract, the mitral valve is pushed closed to prevent backflow into the atrium, and a split second later the aortic valve is pushed open so that the blood can enter the arteries. When the contraction is finished, the blood in the aorta starts falling back, and this pushes the aortic valve closed to prevent backflow into the ventricle. A split second later, the mitral valve is pushed open by the pressure of the blood that constantly enters the atrium from the veins. This permits the left ventricle to fill with blood. The same things are happening at the same time on the right side of the heart. The ventricles fill up and the next cycle begins.

This sequence of events is called the cardiac cycle. There are two parts to the cardiac cycle. The period of ventricular contraction is called systole*, and the period between contractions is called diastole*.

THE HEART NEEDS BLOOD, TOO

Like every other part of the body, the heart itself must have a blood supply system. Circulation to the heart goes along the coronary arteries and veins. There are two small openings in the wall of the aorta, right above the aortic valve. These openings are the beginning of the coronary arteries. The openings are covered up when the valve flaps are open. But as the aortic valve is pushed closed by the pressure of the blood in the arteries after the ventricle has finished its contraction, these openings are uncovered. Now some of the blood pressing down from the aorta and the systemic arteries can flow into the coronary arteries, supplying the heart muscle with oxygen and nutrients. Then this blood is returned along the coronary veins to the right atrium.

WHAT MAKES THE HEART BEAT?

All the events in the cardiac cycle have to be timed very accurately. For example, it would do no good for the ventricle to contract while

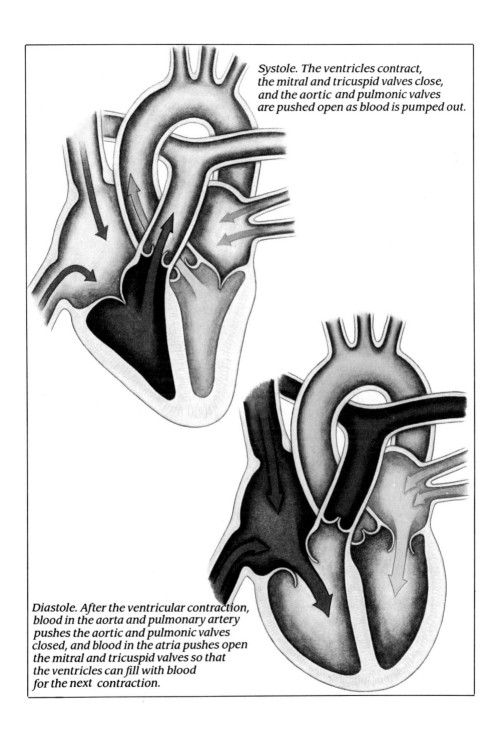

Systole. The ventricles contract, the mitral and tricuspid valves close, and the aortic and pulmonic valves are pushed open as blood is pumped out.

Diastole. After the ventricular contraction, blood in the aorta and pulmonary artery pushes the aortic and pulmonic valves closed, and blood in the atria pushes open the mitral and tricuspid valves so that the ventricles can fill with blood for the next contraction.

it is empty. The ventricular contraction has to take place when the chamber is full, so that the largest amount of blood can be pumped out with each contraction. An electrical impulse-conduction system controls the timing and sequence of events.

Near the top of the right atrium is a special patch of tissue that has a unique job: All by itself, this sinoatrial (SA) node generates regular electrical impulses. The nervous system can make the SA node generate impulses faster or slower, but no "signal" is needed for the SA node to generate impulses at its own rate – that happens automatically.

The electrical impulses are carried very quickly along the conduction system. First, the impulse goes through the right and left atria, causing them to contract. This atrial contraction comes right near the end of diastole. The mitral and tricuspid valves are already open at this point – they opened almost as soon as the last ventricular contraction was over, pushed open by the blood in the atria. Most of that blood entered the ventricle at once, and this atrial contraction simply pushes the last possible amount of blood into the ventricle just before the ventricle contracts.

After the impulse flashes through the atria, it goes to another node, located between the atria and the ventricles, in the septum that divides the left and right sides of the heart. This atrioventricular (AV) node has two jobs.

First, it has to delay the impulse for a moment. Otherwise, the impulse would just go on and cause the ventricles to contract at the same time as the atria were trying to contract. Then the ventricular contraction would close the mitral and tricuspid valves before the atria could pump the last amount of blood down into the ventricles.

Second, the AV node has to be ready to take over for the SA node if the SA node ever stops working. This is a safety feature, because it is absolutely vital for the heart to keep working. The SA node is normally the "pacemaker" for the heart, generating the impulses that cause the heart to pump. But if this pacemaker fails, the AV node will start generating impulses by itself.

After the impulse has been delayed just long enough to allow the atria to contract, the AV node passes the impulse down to the ventricles. The impulse goes through the Bundle of His*, which

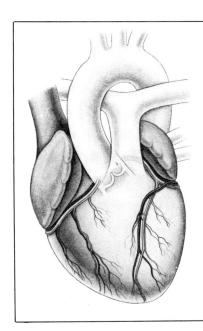

The coronary circulation. In diastole, when the cusps of the aortic valve are pushed closed, the openings of the coronary arteries are uncovered and blood flows in.

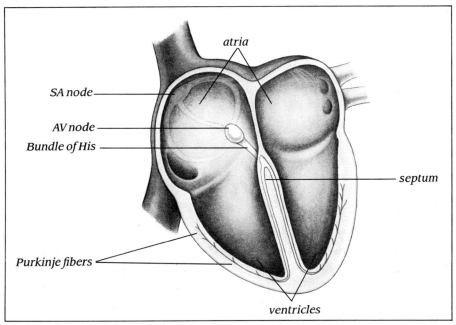

atria

SA node

AV node

Bundle of His

septum

Purkinje fibers

ventricles

The Electrical Impulse Conduction System

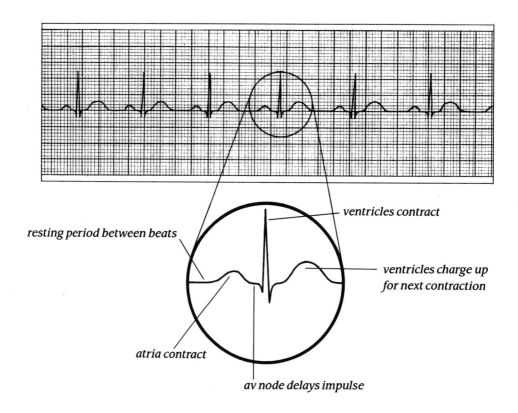

ventricles contract

resting period between beats

ventricles charge up
for next contraction

atria contract

av node delays impulse

A Normal Electrocardiogram

divides into left and right branches that run down either side of the septum between the ventricles. From these pathways, little Purkinje fibers* carry the impulse through the ventricles. The ventricles, in turn, contract when the electrical impulse has stimulated the heart muscle.

The electrocardiogram (ECG) is a device that traces all these electrical impulses as they are conducted through the heart. A doctor can identify many different heart problems from abnormal conduction patterns.

 # 3: HIGH BLOOD PRESSURE

Blood in the arteries presses outward against the walls of the vessels. It is like water inside a garden hose. You can tell that the water is pressing outward because if you punch a small hole in the side of the hose, water will squirt out.

Each time the ventricles contract and pump blood into the arteries, the heart is pushing against the pressure of the blood already in the arteries. The higher the arterial pressure, the harder the heart must push to open the aortic valve and pump blood out. When the pressure from blood inside the arteries is too high, it makes the heart work too hard.

WHAT CONTROLS BLOOD PRESSURE?

The heart, the nervous system, and the kidneys are all involved in controlling blood pressure. The role of the heart is direct. In general, the more blood the heart pumps into the arteries, the higher the pressure.

The nervous system senses changes in blood pressure. As soon as the pressure starts to fall below normal, the heart beats faster and harder (increasing the amount of blood being pumped into the arteries), and the arteries will squeeze down a little. If the pressure rises above normal, the

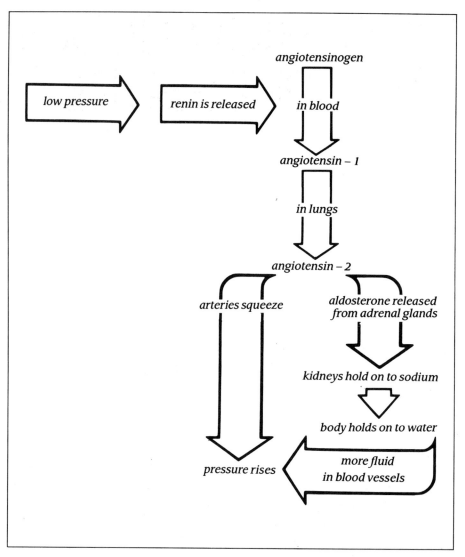

How The Kidneys Raise Blood Pressure

reverse happens. These changes take place from instant to instant, to keep the blood pressure steady. The role of the kidney is more complicated. Special structures can sense changes in the pressure inside certain blood vessels in the kidney. If the pressure in this area falls, the kidney will raise blood pressure all over the body in two ways.

First, the kidney will release a substance called renin* into the blood. Renin changes angiotensinogen* (which is already in the blood) into angiotensin-1. As angiotensin-1 circulates through the body, it passes through the lungs, where it is changed into angiotensin-2, which raises blood pressure by causing the arteries to squeeze down.

Then, angiotensin-2 causes the adrenal glands (which sit right on top of the kidneys) to release a substance called aldosterone*. Aldosterone causes the kidneys to hold on to sodium, and that causes the body to hold on to water. With more water in the body, there will be more fluid in the blood vessels, and the pressure will rise.

WHEN BLOOD PRESSURE IS TOO HIGH

Hypertension (high blood pressure) is one of the most common diseases in the United States. Many people who have hypertension don't know they have it. It doesn't cause pain or any other symptoms – not at first. But after many years, there may be very bad problems.

First, the heart may not be able to keep up the extra effort needed to pump blood out against the high pressure in the arteries. If the heart is unable to pump out its full load of blood with each beat, that means a certain amount of blood is staying in the heart. Then there is less room for the blood returning along the veins into the atrium to enter the ventricle. Finally, just like a traffic jam, blood piles up through the veins, all the way back to the capillaries.

Second, if the heart isn't pumping out the normal amount of blood with each beat, certain parts of the body may not get their full supply of blood. This happens so that the heart and brain can have their full amounts – for these organs cannot survive very long without a good supply of blood. But if circulation to the kidneys is smaller than normal, extra fluid will stay in the body. Even worse, the low pressure inside the kidneys will turn on the renin-angiotensin-aldosterone system to raise the blood pressure and hold on to still more fluid – even though high blood pressure started the whole problem and there is already too much fluid in the body! When the heart is not pumping out enough blood and fluid starts building up everywhere, the result is

23

congestive heart failure. Patients with this problem get very short of breath and bloated with excess fluid. The heart itself gets stretched out of shape, which makes it sluggish and weaker and even less able to pump effectively.

Third, high blood pressure can cause a blood vessel inside the brain to burst open. Most people call this a "stroke," and it can cause death or paralysis. People who have hypertension are much more likely to get strokes than people who have normal blood pressure.

Finally, high blood pressure may increase a person's chance of having coronary artery disease and may also cause kidney failure.

MEASURING BLOOD PRESSURE

Because hypertension can cause such serious problems, it is very important to diagnose it early so that treatment can start. Blood pressure is measured with a device called a sphygmomanometer*. The doctor measures both the systolic pressure (the pressure during the ventricular contraction, as blood is being pumped into the arterial system) and the diastolic pressure (the pressure during the resting period between heartbeats). In many cases the diastolic pressure is considered more important than the systolic pressure.

Blood pressure is given as two numbers, the systolic pressure "over" the diastolic pressure – for example, "one hundred twenty over seventy" (written 120/70). Usually, doctors regard pressures that are constantly above 140/90 as too high.

However, as people get older, it is normal for blood pressure, especially the systolic pressure, to rise, because the arteries get harder and less able to "stretch" under pressure from the blood inside them.

When hypertension is diagnosed, the doctor still has to answer these questions: What has caused the hypertension? Has the high pressure already caused damage to the body? How shall it be treated?

WHAT CAUSES HYPERTENSION?

There are two main types of hypertension. In a few cases, a specific cause can be found. For example, a tumor may be pouring out a substance that raises blood pressure. Or a person may have some blockage in the artery that goes to the kidney. Then the kidney, getting too little blood, turns on its renin-angiotensin-

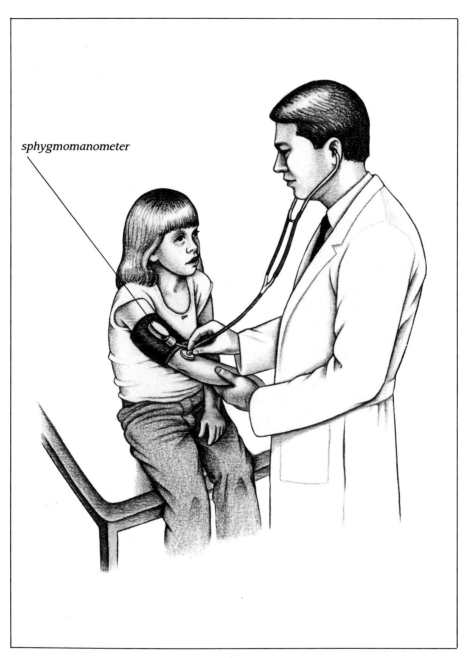

sphygmomanometer

Taking blood pressure is quick and easy.

aldosterone system, and the pressure rises. These cases are called secondary hypertension, because the high blood pressure is caused by something else.

However, most cases are called primary, or "essential," hypertension, because no cause can be found. One theory about primary hypertension has to do with sodium, which is found in salt. Water is drawn toward sodium. So a person who eats too much salt will keep too much water. The excess fluid in the body raises the pressure inside the blood vessels. Not everyone who eats too much salt gets high blood pressure, and some doctors think that the people who develop essential hypertension are those who cannot deal with salt as well as other people. Black people are more likely to develop essential hypertension than white people, but no one is sure why.

TREATMENT

With secondary hypertension, treatment is aimed at the cause. If the cause is a tumor, for example, a surgeon will try to remove it. The surgeon may remove an obstruction in the artery to a kidney or remove an obstruction in the aorta. Once the cause of hypertension has been treated,

the blood pressure should come down.

With primary hypertension, there is no cause that can be eliminated, so treatment is aimed at the high blood pressure itself. There are many ways to lower the blood pressure. People can do some things themselves.

If a person is obese, reducing weight will often lower the blood pressure. (Maintaining proper body weight is very important in preventing and treating any kind of heart disease.) Cigarette smoke causes the arteries to squeeze down, which raises the blood pressure while a person is smoking. The more often a person smokes, the more the pressure will be kept elevated. Doctors aren't sure whether stopping smoking will lower a high blood pressure, but it will certainly make the heart's work easier. And because salt causes the body to hold on to excess water, people can cut down on the amount of salt they eat in their food. Most Americans eat far too much salt, and that is probably one reason why hypertension is such a common disease.

Sometimes, in a mild case of hypertension, these changes in lifestyle will be enough to reduce the pressure. But even if medicine must also be used, these methods are still important.

The most commonly used drugs to treat hypertension are diuretics. They work by causing the kidney to excrete sodium into the urine. Since water is drawn toward sodium, that will draw a lot of water out of the body.

Beta-blockers are also useful in reducing blood pressure. These drugs are believed to work in three ways: by making the heart rate slower, by interfering with renin, and by decreasing the effect of natural substances that tend to constrict small arteries.

Vasodilators work directly on the arteries, to make them relax and stop squeezing down. That reduces the blood pressure quickly, but it may also cause the heart to beat faster.

One of the newest drugs works by stopping the change of angiotensin-1 into angiotensin-2. That removes one of the main substances that cause the arteries to squeeze down.

All these drugs work well, yet hypertension remains a serious problem. Why is that? For the same reason that many people don't even know they have hypertension: the disease causes no pain or other symptoms. So even after being told that they have high blood pressure, some people will just stop taking their medicine because they feel fine. If they stop taking medicine, if they let themselves get overweight, if they eat too much salt, the blood pressure will go right back up. In most cases, the condition has to be treated for the person's entire life. With proper treatment, a person with hypertension can lead an absolutely normal life. Without treatment, over many years, hypertension can lead to congestive heart failure, stroke, and even death.

WHAT ABOUT LOW BLOOD PRESSURE?

There is no such disease as low blood pressure. As long as the heart is pumping out enough blood to meet all the body's needs, there is no harm from having a low blood pressure. It may be a problem in a person who has lost a lot of blood from bleeding or in someone with heart failure. But when no other diseases are present, a low blood pressure is healthy.

27

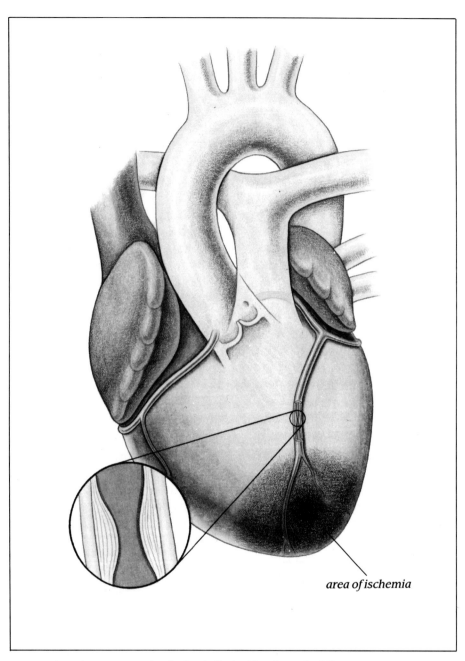

area of ischemia

Atherosclerosis. Coronary circulation is limited by plaque building up inside artery.

4: CORONARY ARTERY DISEASE

Cells in the body need oxygen brought in by the bloodstream. The more work done by the cells in different organs of the body, the more oxygen is needed. Without oxygen, cells die. Because the heart works continuously, it requires a very good blood supply from the coronary arteries. If those vessels do not carry enough blood to bring oxygen to all parts of the heart, the results can be very serious.

POOR CORONARY CIRCULATION

The most common cause of poor circulation through the heart is that the coronary arteries become blocked with hard deposits. This process is called atherosclerosis*. It starts out as a plaque on the inside wall of an artery. At first, the blood just goes right over it. But the plaque gets bigger as more material builds up, until the blood can barely get past it. Then the areas of the heart that are supplied by that coronary artery will not get a full amount of blood and oxygen. Eventually, the artery may become completely plugged up by the deposit.

Scientists are not sure what causes atherosclerosis. However, certain factors are suspected.

Atherosclerosis is more commonly seen in people who smoke, who have high levels of cholesterol*, or high blood pressure. Lack of exercise may also be a factor. In order to minimize the risk, many doctors advise people not to smoke, to get regular exercise, to keep blood pressure under control, and to reduce the amount of meat, eggs, and milk in their diet. Foods that come from animals contain cholesterol and saturated fat, which is also harmful. Fruits, vegetables, and grains contain no cholesterol at all.

ANGINA PECTORIS

When any part of the body does not receive enough oxygen, the condition is called ischemia*. Ischemia in the heart muscle, usually from poor coronary circulation, causes discomfort in the chest (angina pectoris*).

For example, a person may have plaque building up inside one of the coronary arteries. As long as that person is resting, the heart rate is normal and there is still enough blood flowing past the plaque to supply the heart muscle's needs. But during physical activity, such as climbing stairs, the heart will have to beat faster to supply extra blood and oxygen to the muscles doing the extra work. Then the heart, which is also a muscle, will need extra oxygen, because it, too, is doing extra work – but it can't get the extra oxygen it needs because of the plaque inside the coronary artery. Suddenly, the person has an unpleasant feeling in the chest and stops climbing to let the heart slow down. At the normal heart rate, the oxygen supplied by the coronary circulation is enough, and the feeling goes away in a minute or so.

In some people, coronary artery disease gets worse over time. It takes less physical activity to cause chest pain, and it takes longer for the pain to go away. Eventually, they may even have chest pain while they are at rest. These people are in serious danger.

MYOCARDIAL INFARCTION

If a coronary artery is severely blocked, the area of the heart that gets its blood supply from that artery may die from lack of oxygen, while the rest of the heart goes on working. This event is called a myocardial infarction*, or a "heart attack." It usually occurs because of a blood clot* in the narrowed coronary artery. The size and location of an infarction depend on location

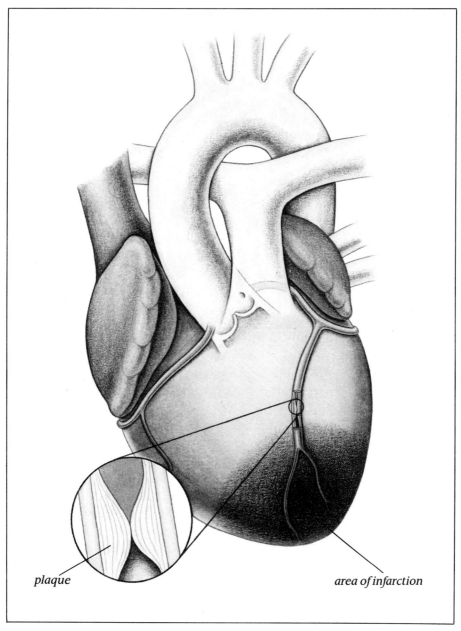

plaque

area of infarction

Myocardial infarction. Lack of blood past plaque results in death of tissue in area affected by lack of circulation.

of the blockage in the coronary artery system. Many patients survive a heart attack when it is diagnosed and treated promptly. But if the area of infarction is very large, the person may die. The ventricles, deprived of oxygen, may begin quivering instead of pumping. This is a medical emergency. It is treated by sending a strong electric shock through the patient's chest, to try to get the heart pumping again. Sometimes the heart just stops completely. Drugs given immediately may get the heart started again – otherwise, the patient is dead.

In patients who survive, there may be permanent damage to the heart. The area of infarction becomes like scar tissue – it is still part of the heart's structure, but that area no longer contracts properly.

DIAGNOSING CORONARY ARTERY DISEASE

A doctor will suspect coronary artery disease from the patient's own description of chest discomfort that comes with physical exertion. An electrocardiogram is usually normal in patients with angina. However, an exercise stress test may reveal coronary artery disease. In this test, an ECG is taken after the person performs a specific kind of exercise, such as running on a treadmill, until the heart is beating at a certain, fast rate. The ECG may then show the pattern for ischemia if there is any problem in the coronary arteries. But even this test is not sensitive enough to detect all cases of coronary artery disease.

In a person who has had a heart attack, the infarction produces a different pattern on the ECG because dead tissue will not conduct electrical impulses at all; in about 75 to 80 percent of people who have had a heart attack, tracings show how the impulses have to go around the area of infarction. A doctor will confirm the diagnosis of myocardial infarction by testing the blood for certain substances that spill out of myocardial cells when the cells are damaged.

Cardiologists – doctors who treat heart disease – sometimes perform special tests to confirm the diagnosis of coronary artery disease. In angiography*, the doctor inserts a thin tube into an artery and threads it back toward the heart. When the tube reaches the area of the aortic valve where the coronary arteries begin, the doctor injects some dye through the tube. The dye enters the coronary arteries, and on an

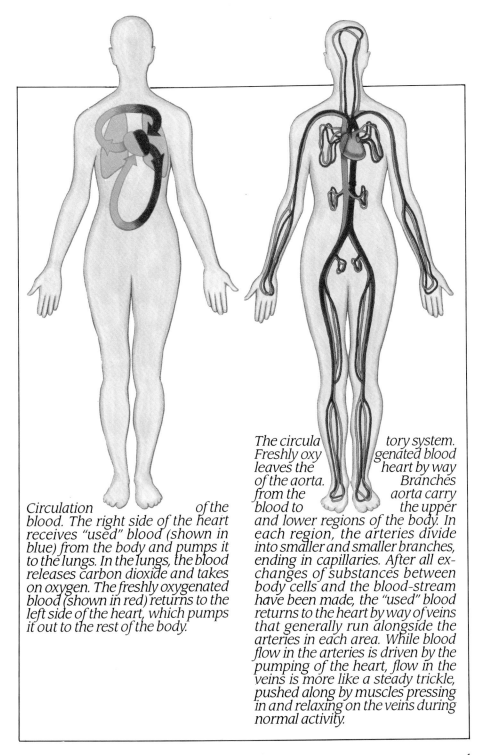

Circulation of the blood. The right side of the heart receives "used" blood (shown in blue) from the body and pumps it to the lungs. In the lungs, the blood releases carbon dioxide and takes on oxygen. The freshly oxygenated blood (shown in red) returns to the left side of the heart, which pumps it out to the rest of the body.

The circula tory system. Freshly oxy genated blood leaves the heart by way of the aorta. Branches from the aorta carry blood to the upper and lower regions of the body. In each region, the arteries divide into smaller and smaller branches, ending in capillaries. After all exchanges of substances between body cells and the blood-stream have been made, the "used" blood returns to the heart by way of veins that generally run alongside the arteries in each area. While blood flow in the arteries is driven by the pumping of the heart, flow in the veins is more like a steady trickle, pushed along by muscles pressing in and relaxing on the veins during normal activity.

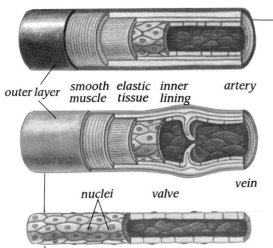

outer layer — smooth muscle — elastic tissue — inner lining — artery

nuclei — valve — vein

capillary

Types of vessels. Arteries (vessels that carry blood away from the heart) have thicker muscular walls than veins (vessels that carry blood back toward the heart). Capillaries are the smallest vessels and have the thinnest walls. They form a bridge between the arteries and the veins throughout the body. All exchanges – of oxygen, nutrients, carbon dioxide, and other waste products – between the bloodstream and body cells take place through the capillaries.

The structure of the heart. "Used" blood from the body enters the right atrium by way of the superior and inferior vena cavae. At the same time, oxygenated blood from the lungs enters the left atrium by way of the pulmonary veins. Blood from the right atrium goes down past the tricuspid valve to the right ventricle, while blood from the left atrium goes down past the mitral valve to the left ventricle. The septum keeps the blood from the left and right sides of the heart from mixing. The right ventricle pumps the "used" blood out past the pulmonic valve into the pulmonary artery, which will carry the blood to the lungs. At the same time, the left ventricle pumps the oxygenated blood out past the aortic valve into the aorta, which is the beginning of the arterial system.

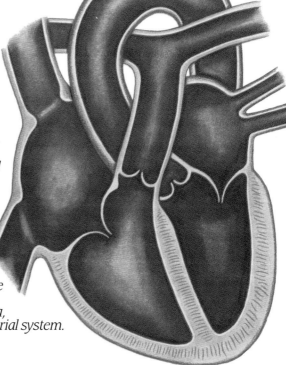

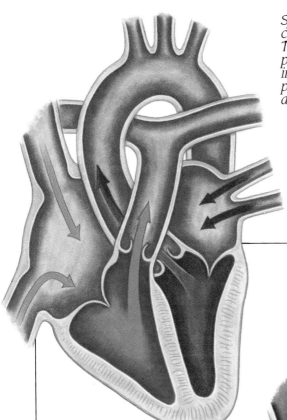

Systole is the part of the cardiac cycle when the ventricles contract. The mitral and tricuspid valves are pushed closed to prevent backflow into the atria, and the aortic and pulmonic valves are pushed open as blood is pumped out.

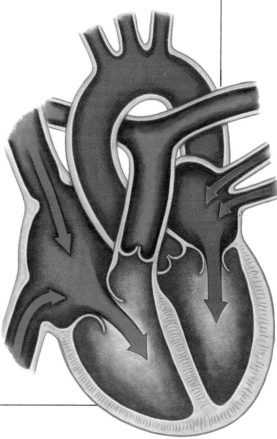

Diastole is the part of the cardiac cycle when the heart rests between contractions. Blood in the aorta and in the pulmonary artery pushes the aortic and pulmonic valves closed to prevent backflow into the ventricles, and blood in the atria pushes open the mitral and tricuspid valves so that the ventricles can fill up for the next contraction.

3

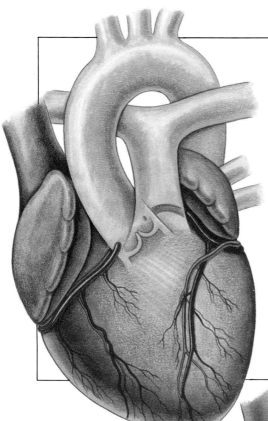

The coronary circulation. The heart muscle needs its own circulation. During diastole, when the cusps of the aortic valve are pushed down, the openings of the coronary arteries are uncovered, allowing oxygenated blood in the aorta to flow in. As the ventricles contract, "used" blood in the coronary veins is pushed toward an opening into the right atrium.

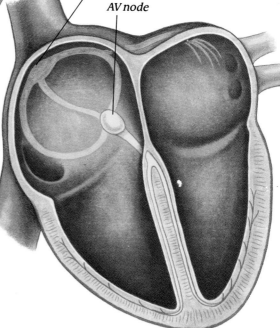

SA node

AV node

The impulse conduction system. The sinoatrial (SA) node produces impulses all by itself. The impulse goes through the atria, causing them to contract. The atrioventricular (AV) node delays the impulse, giving the atria time to finish pushing blood down into the ventricles. Then the impulse goes through the ventricles, causing them to contract (this is systole) and pump blood out of the heart.

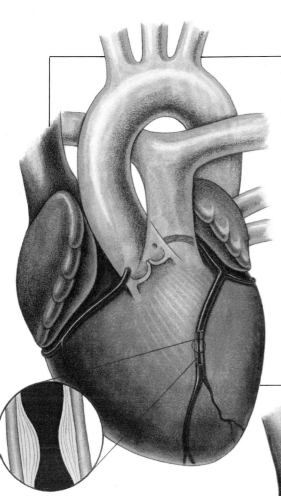

Atherosclerosis. Coronary circulation is limited by plaque building inside the artery. People who have high levels of cholesterol in their blood are more likely to develop this condition.

Myocardial infarction. When blood cannot get through the coronary arteries (often because plaque is blocking the vessel), the affected area of the heart dies from the lack of circulation.

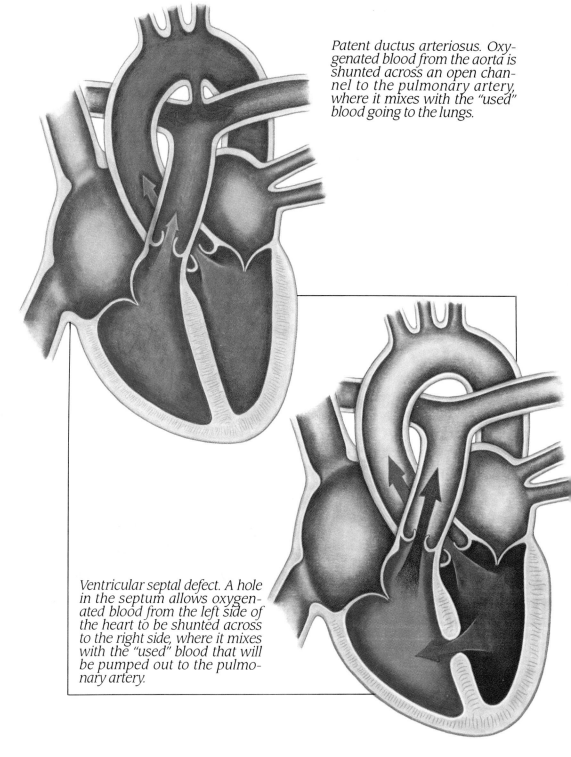

Patent ductus arteriosus. Oxygenated blood from the aorta is shunted across an open channel to the pulmonary artery, where it mixes with the "used" blood going to the lungs.

Ventricular septal defect. A hole in the septum allows oxygenated blood from the left side of the heart to be shunted across to the right side, where it mixes with the "used" blood that will be pumped out to the pulmonary artery.

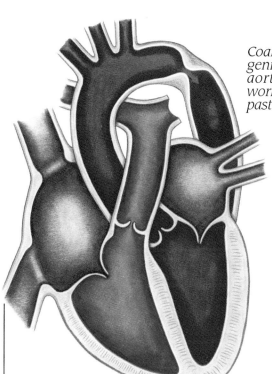

Coarctation of the aorta is a congenital area of narrowing in the aorta. The left ventricle has to work much harder to push blood past the narrowed area.

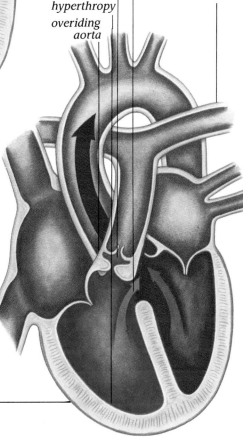

septal defect
valve stenosis
hyperthropy
overiding
aorta

Tetralogy of Fallot is a combination of four defects in the heart: a ventricular septal defect, pulmonic valve stenosis, right ventricular hypertrophy, and an "overriding" aorta (where the aorta arises from both the right and left ventricles instead of from the left ventricle alone). Cyanosis results from "used" blood from the right ventricle being shunted to the left side, where it mixes with the oxygenated blood entering the arteries. "Used" blood enters the arteries in two ways: through the ventricular septal defect and directly from the right ventricle into the overriding aorta.

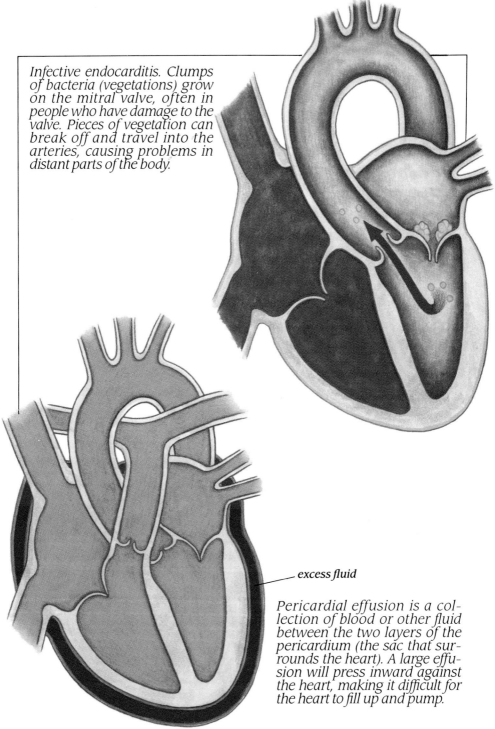

Infective endocarditis. Clumps of bacteria (vegetations) grow on the mitral valve, often in people who have damage to the valve. Pieces of vegetation can break off and travel into the arteries, causing problems in distant parts of the body.

excess fluid

Pericardial effusion is a collection of blood or other fluid between the two layers of the pericardium (the sac that surrounds the heart). A large effusion will press inward against the heart, making it difficult for the heart to fill up and pump.

X-ray, the dye will show where the blockage is.

In another test a radioactive substance is injected into a vein. When the substance reaches the heart, the doctor can use special equipment to see areas of scar tissue, ischemia, or other problems.

TREATING CORONARY ARTERY DISEASE

The same healthy lifestyle that may prevent coronary artery disease is an important part of treatment. Keeping body weight down, avoiding foods with cholesterol and saturated fat, and avoiding smoking are all vital in treating coronary artery disease. Exercise is still important, too, but a doctor will have to advise the patient with coronary artery disease what type of exercise to do and how much is good.

Doctors may also prescribe certain medications to treat angina pectoris. Nitroglycerin works by making the blood vessels open up wider. That helps in three ways. Blood pressure in the arteries drops, so that the heart doesn't have to work as hard to pump blood out. Some blood stays in the veins, so that less blood returns to the heart to be pumped out. And the coronary arteries themselves open up a little to improve coronary circulation.

Beta-blocker drugs prevent the heart rate from rising too high with exercise. By keeping down the amount of work being done by the heart, they ensure that the amount of oxygen needed by the heart won't go much higher than the amount that can be supplied by the coronary circulation.

In some cases of angina pectoris, surgery may be necessary. A section of a vein from the patient's leg is taken out and used to bypass (go around) the blocked area of the coronary arteries. This often makes patients feel better and, in a small number of carefully selected cases, may let the patient live longer. A newer technique is to widen a narrow coronary artery by expanding a small balloon at the end of a tube that has been threaded into the artery.

AFTER A HEART ATTACK

A person who has just had a myocardial infarction must be treated in the hospital. This person needs rest, oxygen, medicine for pain, and a special diet. Also, an infarction can lead to serious complications, and a doctor must watch for them and treat them. For example, the area of infarction may affect the impulse-conduction system in the ventricles, interfering with the rhythm of the heart.

Congestive heart failure may develop after a myocardial infarction. The damaged area can't do its share of the work, so the heart can't pump out as much blood as before. As we saw in Chapter 3, the patient becomes short of breath and may retain fluid. The treatment is to get rid of the excess fluid (with diuretics), to reduce the work load of the heart (with drugs that open up the blood vessels), and in some cases, to make the heart pump more strongly (with a drug called digitalis).

In some patients, even more serious complications can occur. The wall of the heart, in the area of the infarction, may balloon out (this is called an aneurysm*) or even burst open.

When the patient recovers from a myocardial infarction, a full program of rehabilitation begins. In the past, people thought that it was dangerous to exercise. Now, carefully controlled regular exercise and returning to work are part of rehabilitation. The doctor will control the patient's blood pressure and advise the patient to lose excess weight, not to smoke, and to avoid foods high in saturated fat and cholesterol.

5: CONGENITAL DEFECTS OF THE HEART

Congenital means "existing from birth." Compared to heart conditions that are acquired during life, congenital conditions are rare. These anatomical defects fall into two main groups: conditions that allow abnormal mixing of blood between the left and right sides of the heart, and conditions that do not involve any such mixing, but may obstruct blood flow.

In the first group, blood moves across an abnormal opening, either from left to right or from right to left. Movement of blood directly from one side of the heart to the other is called a shunt. Blood is shunted from the side of the heart where the pressure is higher to the side where the pressure is lower. Usually, the left side of the heart has higher pressure than the right side. Then if there is an abnormal opening (either a hole in the septum between the atria or between the ventricles, or an open connection between the aorta and the pulmonary artery), freshly oxygenated blood from the left side is shunted to the right side, where it mixes with the "used" blood about to go to the lungs.

Conditions in which the pressure is higher on the right side are less common and generally more serious. "Used" blood from the right side is shunted to the left side, where it mixes with the freshly oxygenated blood about to go out into the arteries. If the abnormal opening is big and a large amount of "used" blood goes out into the arteries, a baby's skin will have a blue tone (cyanosis*). This is because "used" blood is very dark compared to the bright red color of freshly oxygenated blood.

In the second group, there is no mixing of "used" and freshly oxygenated blood. Most of these defects involve areas in the heart that are too tight and narrow, making it hard for blood to flow past.

All these congenital defects make the heart work too hard. When there is a shunt, the side of the heart that receives blood from the other side has to work harder to pump out the extra volume. When there is a tight or narrow passage, the heart has to work harder to push to blood past. If the condition is severe and is not corrected, the heart will not be able to keep up extra effort, and congestive heart failure will develop, often resulting in death.

Most often, congenital defects in the heart occur by themselves. But in about one out of five cases, the heart defect is just one of several congenital problems. For example, babies born with Down syndrome are mentally retarded, and many of them also have congenital heart defects.

SEPTAL DEFECTS
A hole in the septum between the left and right atria is called an atrial septal defect. Blood is shunted from left to right. If the hole is small, it causes no problems. But if a large amount of blood is being shunted, the right side of the heart has to handle more than it is designed to handle. Like any muscle that is exercised, the right ventricle will become hypertrophied* (enlarged) as it is forced to handle the extra load – but there is a limit. After that, the heart will fail. To avoid that, doctors can perform an operation to close the hole.

Ventricular septal defect – a hole in the septum between the left and right ventricles – is usually more serious. Again, the right side of the heart is forced to handle a larger volume of blood than it is meant to handle. The hole will close by itself during

36

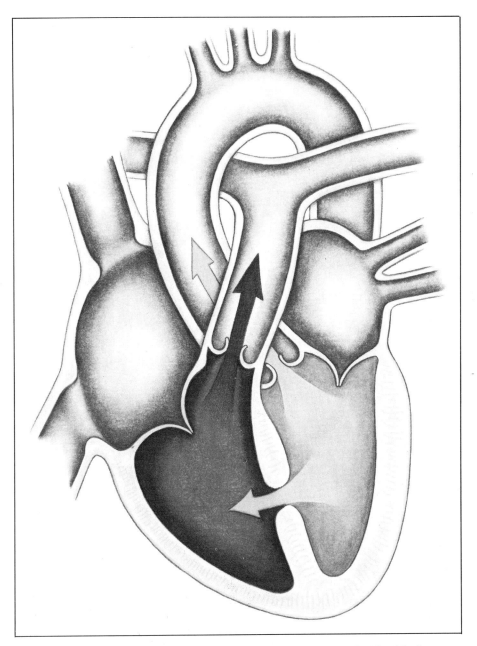

Ventricular septal defect. Oxygenated blood is shunted from the left side of the heart to the right side.

early childhood in fewer than half the cases. If the hole is big and it does not close by itself, an operation may be required.

In some cases of ventricular septal defect, a surprising thing happens after a while. The direction of the shunt reverses. When a shunt that had been going from left to right changes and goes from right to left, it is called Eisenmenger's syndrome*. The pressure in the pulmonary artery gets very high because the small blood vessels in the lungs become narrow. This narrowing places a strain on the right ventricle that is trying to pump blood through the lungs. Because the tricuspid valve prevents backflow into the right atrium, the only way the blood in the right ventricle can go is through the septal defect, into the left ventricle. Eisenmenger's syndrome can also occur in cases of atrial septal defect, but it is less common. Once Eisenmenger's syndrome has occurred, it is too late to operate on the septal defect – because then closing the hole would leave no way for the blood to get out of the heart.

PATENT DUCTUS ARTERIOSUS

Before a baby is born, the lungs do not work at all because the fetus is not breathing air. An open vessel connects the aorta and the pulmonary artery at this time, so that blood from the right side of the fetal heart can go into the aorta instead of going to the lungs. Normally, this ductus arteriosus* closes up shortly after birth. If it remains patent (open), the higher pressure in the aorta will shunt blood into the pulmonary artery. This is another left-to-right shunt. Eisenmenger's syndrome can also occur with this defect. Doctors can easily recognize this abnormality and will operate on almost all patients who suffer from it.

TETRALOGY OF FALLOT

Named after a French doctor who first described it, Tetralogy of Fallot* is a combination of four congenital problems in the heart. The main problem is narrowing below the pulmonic valve. The right ventricle must work hard to try to push blood past the obstruction and out into the pulmonary artery. This effort creates the second problem, enlargement of the right ventricle. The third problem is a ventricular septal defect. Because it is too hard to push blood past the narrowed pulmonic valve, some of the "used" blood in the

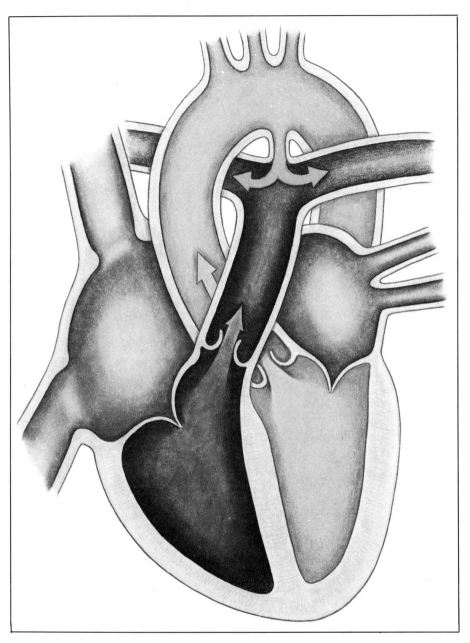

Patent ductus arteriosus. Oxygenated blood is shunted from the aorta to the pulmonary artery.

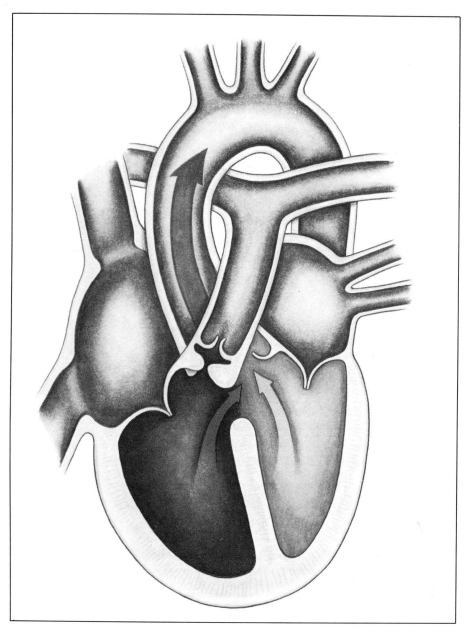

Tetralogy of Fallot. Cyanosis results from "used" blood from right side of heart entering the arteries, both through the ventricular septal defect and directly into the aorta.

right ventricle will be shunted to the left ventricle, causing cyanosis. The fourth problem is that the aorta is positioned too far to the right side of the heart, so that it arises from both the right and left ventricles, instead of from the left ventricle only. This allows more "used" blood from the right side to enter the aorta and the arterial system. Tetralogy of Fallot is the most common congenital defect that causes cyanosis.

Although a great deal of blood is being shunted from right to left, very little can get past the obstruction in the outflow part of the right ventricle. The treatment is surgical – the surgeon can create an opening between the pulmonary artery and one of the arteries that branch from the aorta. This opening allows some blood to be shunted into the pulmonary artery system, so that it can go to the lungs. Then, after the shunted blood dumps its carbon dioxide and picks up fresh oxygen, it returns from the lungs to the left side of the heart. In this way, the left ventricle has at least some oxygenated blood to pump out to the rest of the body.

VALVE STENOSIS

Pulmonic valve stenosis* (tightness, narrowing) is another type of congenital heart defect. The right ventricle enlarges as it tries to push blood past the narrowed valve and out into the pulmonary artery. If the condition is bad enough, heart failure will result. To avoid that, an operation can be done to widen the valve opening. Sometimes, pulmonic valve stenosis occurs along with an atrial septal defect. Then blood in the right atrium is shunted across to the left atrium, because that is an easier path than trying to enter the stiff, hypertrophied right ventricle. The result is cyanosis and extra work for the left side of the heart.

Congenital aortic stenosis is a common type of congenital heart disease. There may be only two valve cusps instead of the normal three. The left side of the heart has to work harder to push blood past the obstruction. The result is left ventricular hypertrophy. The condition may only become known in middle age, as the patient develops heart failure, fainting, and ischemia in the heart muscle.

Surgical correction of the obstruction in pulmonic or aortic valve stenosis is possible. In very young children, the valve can be widened. Later, especially in aortic stenosis, the valve may have to be replaced.

COARCTATION OF THE AORTA

Picture an hourglass. It is like a tube that is pinched and narrow in one place, so that sand runs through it very slowly. Coarctation* means that the aorta is pinched and narrow in one place, and blood flows past it very slowly. It is something like aortic valve stenosis, except that the tight spot is up in the aorta, beyond the valve. And like valve stenosis, it makes the left ventricle work too hard, and that often leads to heart failure. The treatment for this congenital defect is surgery to remove the pinched section of the aorta.

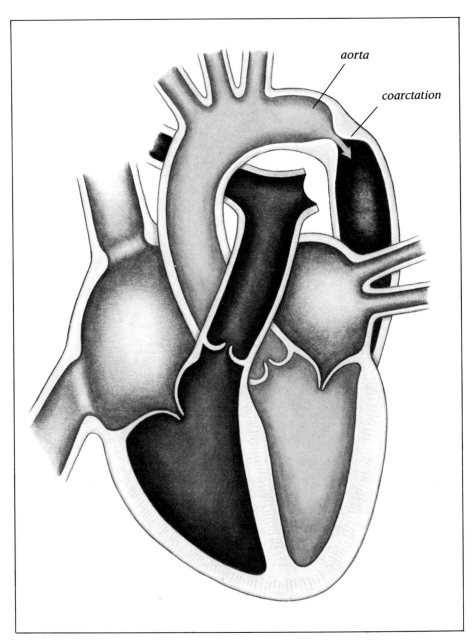

aorta

coarctation

Coarctation of the Aorta

6: INFECTIONS OF THE HEART

If an infection enters the blood from anywhere in the body, it will reach the heart. Most often, the germ will just pass through. An infection inside the heart occurs mainly where there is a place for the germs to settle on and grow – usually on a misshapen heart valve, a ventricular septal defect, or a patent ductus arteriosus. The misshapen valve may have been damaged by disease, or it may have been abnormal from birth.

RHEUMATIC FEVER

In the past, rheumatic fever was the most common cause of valve damage. It occurs less often today. This disease is not an infection itself, but it sometimes comes after throat infection caused by a particular germ called Group A beta-hemolytic streptococcus. As the body's immune system fights this germ, many parts of the body also become targets of the immune system. Occasionally, the immune system acts against the body's own tissues, and that is called autoimmunity (immunity against self). The heart is one of the main targets of an autoimmune reaction following this streptococcus infection, but the lungs, skin, and nervous system may also be affected. Rheumatic fever gets its name because it also causes fever and pain in the joints.

The treatment is aspirin, to relieve fever and joint pain; penicillin, to kill any remaining streptococcus germs; and corticosteroids, to control inflammation. Patients with acute rheumatic fever should take penicillin for many years to prevent streptococcal infections from returning.

Acute rheumatic fever causes myocarditis, which is inflammation of the heart muscle and the mitral and aortic valves. Another complication of rheumatic fever is permanent damage to one or more heart valves, especially the mitral valve. This occurs as years pass and scarring takes place.

A doctor can tell that a valve has been damaged by listening to the heart with a stethoscope*. Normally, blood flowing past a valve makes no sound. But if the valve does not open or close completely, the flow of blood is disturbed, and this creates a soft sound called a murmur.

The mitral valve should be closed during systole. If it is incompetent (if it cannot close completely), some blood will go back up into the atrium as the ventricle contracts, creating a murmur during systole. The valve should be open during diastole. If it is narrowed – stenotic – the blood flowing from the atrium to fill the ventricle will cause a murmur in diastole. With either mitral incompetence or stenosis, the heart is forced to work much harder than normal, and that may lead to congestive heart failure. The aortic valve may also be damaged, resulting in stenosis or incompetence.

Not all murmurs come from rheumatic heart disease. Heart valves may also be damaged if the heart becomes stretched out of shape from congestive heart failure, or a defective valve may be a congenital condition. Many children have "innocent murmurs" that cause no problems and go away as the children grow up. The most common cause of mitral valve leakage is called prolapse, in which the valve cusps drift back into the left atrium during systole. If the leakage is bad, the valve must be surgically replaced.

Not all cases of myocarditis result from rheumatic heart disease, either. It may be caused by viruses or certain rare diseases. To get a better picture of valve disease, doctors use echocardiography, in which sound waves are bounced off the valve, and Doppler studies, which can record the amount and rate of blood flow past a valve.

INFECTIVE ENDOCARDITIS

A damaged heart valve is a place where germs in the blood can settle in and grow, forming large "vegetations" on the valve. This condition is called infective endocarditis*. It is often caused by infections from other areas of the body, carried to the heart by the blood. But a number of cases are caused by people using dirty needles to inject themselves with illegal drugs.

Pieces of vegetation may break off from the infected valve and travel along the arteries. If the fragment gets stuck in a vital organ such as the brain, it can be fatal.

Infective endocarditis must be treated quickly, with high doses of antibiotics. If the valve is too badly infected, it has to be replaced, usually with an artificial valve. Unfortunately, replacement valves themselves are often the target of infection.

To protect against endocarditis, patients must take antibiotics in a preventive way. For example, when a dentist works on a person's teeth and gums, germs from the mouth can enter the bloodstream. People who have valve damage must take antibiotics before and after going to a dentist or having certain medical procedures done. These people are always at high risk of developing infective endocarditis. And with each recurrent case, it is harder to treat and more likely to be fatal.

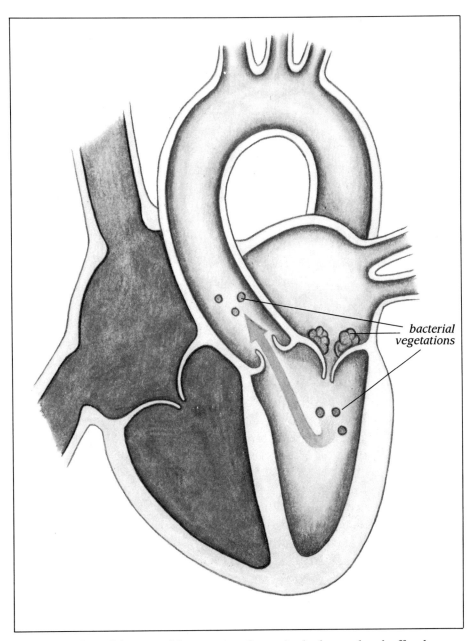

bacterial vegetations

Infective endocarditis. Bacterial vegetations from mitral valve can break off and travel into the arteries.

7: PERICARDIAL DISEASES

The heart is wrapped up in a two-layer coat called the pericardium*. The tough outer layer holds the heart steady inside the chest. The inner layer is a thin membrane that sticks to the heart itself. A film of fluid between the two layers lets them glide smoothly over each other as the heart fills up and contracts.

Diseases of the pericardium involve inflammation, excess fluid between the two layers, and abnormal growths.

PERICARDITIS

The ending -itis means "inflammation," a painful process that takes place when the body's tissues are damaged. Inflammation of the pericardium may be caused by infection, physical injury, harmful substances in the blood, radiation, or tumors. It may also be caused by an autoimmune process (see Chapter 6). Pericarditis is seen with a number of autoimmune diseases, including rheumatic fever and certain forms of arthritis, such as lupus and rheumatoid arthritis.

Pericarditis causes pain in the chest, especially when the person takes a deep breath; a particular pattern on the ECG; and a

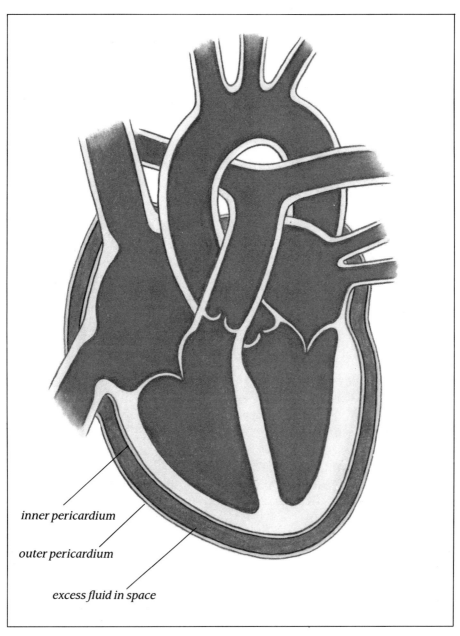

inner pericardium

outer pericardium

excess fluid in space

Pericardial Effusion

rubbing sound as the heart beats, caused by the two layers of the inflamed pericardium scraping against each other. The doctor hears this sound by listening through a stethoscope.

Whatever caused the pericarditis should be treated, if possible. But there is no specific cure for the pericarditis itself. If the cause can be treated, the problem will usually clear up. Doctors prescribe medicine to relieve pain; in very bad cases, they prescribe corticosteroids to fight inflammation.

In some cases of pericarditis, the inflammation destroys the space between the two layers. After several months, what is left is a tight coat of scar tissue that surrounds the heart. This is called constrictive pericarditis. The heart cannot open up all the way during diastole. Usually, a surgeon has to operate to remove the scarred pericardium. The heart can still work, even without its pericardium.

EXCESS FLUID

Another complication of pericarditis is that a large amount of fluid may accumulate between the two layers of the pericardium. This is called a pericardial effusion*. If enough fluid builds up, it will press inward against the heart. Then the heart has less room to open up and fill with blood during diastole. When pericardial fluid presses inward against the heart and doesn't let it fill up completely, it is called cardiac tamponade*. Tamponade most often develops after surgery or some other physical injury, but it can also happen with pericarditis from other causes.

Cardiac tamponade is a medical emergency. The doctor must drain the fluid from inside the pericardium so that the heart can beat freely. Usually, this is done by carefully sticking a needle in through the outer layer and drawing out the fluid. This procedure is called pericardiocentesis*.

CYSTS AND TUMORS

A cyst is a pocket of fluid, completely enclosed. A cyst in the pericardium does not cause any real problems, but it can be seen on an X-ray of the chest. On an X-ray, it would look like something sticking out on the side of the heart. That is also what a tumor or a ventricular aneurysm looks like (see Chapter 4).

A tumor is an abnormal growth. Most pericardial tumors start somewhere else in the chest and spread to the pericardium. Tumors that start in the pericardium are rare. These are almost always malignant growths — a form of cancer. They often cause a pericardial effusion, and they can be seen on an Xray of the chest.

8: ADVANCES IN TREATING HEART DISEASE

Because heart disease is such a big problem in the United States, a lot of research is done to find better ways to diagnose and treat it. We now have very effective drugs to treat hypertension, congestive heart failure, and dangerous problems in impulse conduction. We have new ways to see the heart as it works.

But the most dramatic advances have been in cardiac surgery. It has been many years since artificial pacemakers were first used for patients with very slow heart rates. Now,

pacemakers are common. Some doctors think that the surgical operations being tested at present will become just as common in the future.

Already there have been over a thousand human heart transplants since the first one done by Dr. Christiaan Barnard in 1967. Many of these patients have lived for several years after surgery. In 1983, a mechanical heart was used to replace a human heart for the first time. That patient lived for only a few months. In 1984, a second patient was given a mechanical heart, and more such operations have been done since. At this time, the mechanical heart is still considered an experiment, but the doctors who are doing the operation think that it will someday become routine.

In 1984, a very unusual experiment was conducted on a baby girl who had been born with a defective heart: Doctors cut the heart out of a living baboon and transplanted it into the girl. She lived just three weeks. There was a great deal of argument over this experiment. Many people, including some doctors, felt that it was wrong to try this experiment when a human heart might have been found.

Questions about medical research are complex. We all want to improve human health, and research sometimes produces new ways to save lives. But research is very expensive, and many doctors now feel that we could save even more lives by preventing disease than by learning new ways to cure it.

Fortunately, heart disease – the number-one killer – is very often preventable. If people would avoid smoking; get plenty of exercise; and reduce the amount of salt, cholesterol, and saturated fat in their diets, a lot of heart disease could be prevented. A healthy lifestyle does not guarantee a person won't get heart disease, but it certainly lowers the risk.

The question is this: Which is a greater advance – improving heart transplants and mechanical hearts, or preventing heart disease? What do you think?

GLOSSARY

Aldosterone *(al-DOSS-ter-own).* A hormone from the adrenal glands. It causes the kidneys to keep sodium in the body.

Aneurysm *(AN-yur-iz-im).* A weak area that has ballooned out in a muscular structure.

Angina pectoris *(an-JY-na PECK-tor-iss).* Pain in the chest from poor coronary circulation.

Angiography *(an-jee-OGG-ra-fee).* A method of seeing the inside of blood vessels by injecting a dye that shows up on an X-ray.

Angiotensinogen *(AN-jee-o-ten-SIN-o-jen).* A substance in the blood, converted by *renin* to angiotensin-1 (AN-jee-o-TEN-sin), which is converted to angiotensin-2, which raises blood pressure and causes the adrenal glands to release *aldosterone.*

Aorta *(a-OR-ta).* The main trunk of the arterial "tree." It arises from the left *ventricle.*

Atherosclerosis *(AH-thur-o-skler-O-sis).* A buildup of plaque on the inner lining of the arteries. The general term for hardening of the arteries from any cause is arteriosclerosis (ar-TEER-ee-o-skler-O-sis).

Atrium *(A-tree-um).* The upper chamber of the heart on either side. Plural is atria.

Cholesterol *(ko-LESS-ter-ol).* A substance manufactured by the body and also found in meats, eggs, and dairy foods. It seems to play a role in the development of *atherosclerosis.*

Clot *(klott).* A clump of blood cells.

Coarctation *(KO-ark-TAY-shin).* A congenital defect in which the *aorta* is pinched and narrow in one place.

Cyanosis *(SY-a-NO-sis).* A bluish color in the skin, caused by dark, "used" blood entering the arteries.

Diastole *(die-AS-toll-ee).* The portion of the cardiac cycle between heartbeats. Adjective is diastolic (DIE-as-TOLL-ick).

Ductus arteriosus *(DUCK-tus ar-teer-ee-O-suss).* A channel between the *aorta* and the pulmonary artery. It is open during fetal life and is supposed to close after birth.

Effusion *(ee-FYOO-zhin).* An abnormal leakage of fluid that collects in a space, such as the space inside the *pericardium.*

Eisenmenger's syndrome *(EYE-zen-MENG-erz).* The change that sometimes occurs when a shunt that had been left-to-right reverses direction and becomes right-to-left.

Endocarditis *(EN-doh-kar-DIE-tiss).* Inflammation of the inner lining of the heart, generally from infection.

His, Bundle of *(HISS).* Part of the impulse conduction system in the heart. It receives the impulse from the atrioventricular node and sends it down branches that run down either side of the septum.

Hypertrophied *(high-PER-tro-feed).* Enlarged, thickened, stiffened; a condition that results from forcing a muscle to work very hard.

Ischemia *(iss-KEE-mee-a).* Lack of oxygen in some part of the body. In the heart, it is usually due to coronary artery disease.

Myocardial infarction *(MY-o-KAR-dee-al in-FARK-shin).* A heart attack. Myocardial refers to the muscle tissue of the heart, and infarction refers to death of tissue.

Pericardiocentesis *(PER-i-KAR-dee-o-sen-TEE-sis).* A procedure in which a needle is inserted into the space inside the *pericardium.*

Pericardium *(PER-i-KAR-dee-um).* The outer wrapping around the heart. It has two layers.

Purkinje fibers *(per-KIN-jee).* Part of the impulse conduction system in the heart. These fibers distribute the impulse throughout the *ventricles.*

Renin *(REE-nin).* A substance released by the kidney when blood pressure inside the kidney is low. It converts *angiotensinogen* in the blood into angiotensin-1.

Sphygmomanometer *(SFIG-mo-ma-NOM-i-ter).* A device used to measure blood pressure.

Stenosis *(ste-NO-sis)*. A tight or narrow opening. Stenosis of the heart valves can be a congenital condition, or it can result from inflammation that leaves the valve too stiff to open completely. Adjective is stenotic (ste-NOT-ick).

Stethoscope *(STETH-a-skope)*. A device used to listen to sounds inside the body, such as the sounds made by the heart as it beats.

Systole *(SIS-toll-ee)*. The portion of the cardiac cycle when the heart is actually beating (that is, when the *ventricles* are contracting). Adjective is systolic (sis-TOLL-ick).

Tamponade *(TAM-po-NODD)*. Pressure that squeezes an organ. Cardiac tamponade occurs when there is so much excess fluid in the pericardial space that it presses inward against the heart.

Tetralogy of Fallot *(tet-RALL-o-jee, fah-LO)*. A congenital combination of four defects in the heart. It is the most common cardiac cause of cyanosis in newborn babies.

Tricuspid *(try-KUSS-pid)*. The valve between the right *atrium* and right *ventricle*. It has three cusps (flaps).

Ventricle *(VEN-tri-kill)*. The lower chamber of the heart on either side. The ventricles are the pumping chambers of the heart. Adjective is ventricular (ven-TRICK-yoo-ler).

INDEX

mechanical, 52-53
structure of the, 14-15
transplants, 52-53
Heart muscle, 30, 36, 41
inflammation of the, 45
Hypertension, 23-24, 26-27, 52
Hypertrophied, 36

Mechanical heart, 52-53
Medical research, 53
Mitral valve, 14-18
inflammation, 45
Murmur, 45
Myocardial infarction, 30-34
Myocarditis, 45

Immune system, 44
Impulse-conduction system, 18-20, 34
Infections, 44-48
Inferior vena cava, 12, 15
Inflammation, 45
pericardial, 48, 50
Intestine, 12
Ischemia, 30, 32-33, 41

Nervous system, 18, 21, 44
Nitroglycerin, 33
Nutrients, 9, 12, 16

Joints, 45

Obesity, 26
Oxygen, 9-10, 12, 16, 41
coronary artery disease and, 29-30, 32-33

Kidneys, 12
blood pressure and, 21-24, 26-27

Pacemaker, 18, 52
Patent ductus arteriosus, 38-39, 44
Penicillin, 45
Pericardial effusion, 49-51
Pericarditis, 48-50
Pericardium, 48
Plaque, 28-31
Prolapse, 45
Pulmonary artery, 12, 14-17
congenital heart defects and, 35, 38-39, 41
Pulmonary circulation, 14
Pulmonary veins, 12, 14-15

Life-style, 7-8, 33, 53
hypertension and, 26
Lungs, 9-12, 14, 23, 38, 44, *see also* Pulmonary
Lupus, 48

Pulmonic valve, 15-17
  stenosis, 41
  Tetralogy of Fallot and, 38
Purkinje fibers, 19-20

Radiation, 48
Renin, 22-24
Research, 53
Rheumatic fever, 44-46, 48
Rheumatoid arthritis, 48

Salt, 26-27, 53
Saturated fat, 30, 33-34, 53
Septum, 14, 18-20
  defects of the, 35-38, 40, 44
Shunt, 35-39, 41
Sinoatrial (SA) node, 18-19
Skin, 44
Smoking, 8, 26, 53
  coronary artery disease and, 30, 33
Sodium, 23, 26-27
Sphygmomanometer, 24-25
Stenosis, 41-42, 45
Stethoscope, 45, 50
Streptococcus, 44
Stroke, 24, 27
Superior vena cava, 12, 15
Surgery, 33, 52-53
Systemic circulation, 14
Systemic veins, 14
Systole, 16-17, 45
Systolic pressure, 24

Tetralogy of Fallot, 38, 40-41
Transplants, 52-53
Tricuspid valve, 14-15, 18, 38
Tumors, 24, 26, 48, 50-51

Urine, 27

Valves, 14-18
  congenital heart disease and, 38, 41-42
  heart infections and, 44-46
Vasodilators, 27
Veins, 12-14, 16, 23
Ventricles, 14-20
  blood pressure and, 21, 23
  congenital heart defects and, 35-38, 40-41
  heart attack and, 32, 34
Ventricular aneurysm, 50

Waste products, 9, 12
Water, 23, 26-27
Weight, 26-27, 33-34

X-ray, 33, 50-51

ABOUT THE AUTHOR

Steven Tiger is a graduate of Brooklyn College and the Physician Assistant Program of Touro College, New York City. Formerly in clinical practice as a physician assistant, he has been editing and writing for numerous medical journals and is also a guest lecturer in medical physiology at the Physician Assistant Program, The Brooklyn Hospital / Long Island University. He is the author of *Arthritis* in the Understanding Disease series.